DUDLEY SCHOOLS
LIBRARY SERVICE

KU-099-332

Schools Library and Information Services

S00000670445

MUSICAL INSTRUMENTS OF THE WORLD

Sound Effects

M. J. Knight

W

FRANKLIN WATTS

LONDON•SYDNEY

 An Appleseed Editions book

First published in 2005 by Franklin Watts
96 Leonard Street, London, EC2A 4XD

Franklin Watts Australia
45-51 Huntley Street, Alexandria, NSW 2015

© 2005 Appleseed Editions

Created by Appleseed Editions Ltd,
Well House, Friars Hill, Guestling, East Sussex, TN35 4ET

Designed by Helen James

All rights reserved. No part of this publication may be reproduced, stored in a
retrieval system or transmitted in any form or by any means, electronic, mechanical,
photocopying, recording or otherwise, without prior permission of the publisher.

ISBN 0 7496 5848 7

A CIP catalogue for this book is available from the British Library.

Photographs by Corbis (Dave Bartruff, Annie Griffiths Belt, Richard Bickel, Owen
Franken, John Gillmoure, John Van Hasselt, Hulton-Deutsch Collection, Bob Krist,
Gabe Palmer, Royalty-Free, Paul Schermeister, Phil Schermeister, David Turnley,
Nevada Wier), The Lebrecht Collection

Printed in Thailand

DUDLEY PUBLIC LIBRARIES

L 47951

670445 | SCH

J 785

Contents

Introducing sound effects

sound effects   sound effects   sound effects   sound effects

This book is about musical instruments which are used to make sound effects. You can hear sound effects on radio programmes, in television and film soundtracks and in the theatre.

Composers include sound effects in the music they write to change the mood, to surprise their listeners, or to soothe them. Some are created to imitate natural sounds, such as the crash of thunder, rain falling, or the clopping of horses' hoofs.

This smiling Cuban musician is playing the maracas.

Many of the instruments used to create sound effects are percussion instruments. They are sounded by hitting, shaking or scraping them.

People all over the world have played musical instruments to create sound effects for thousands of years. They range from pieces of wood banged together, to unusual sounds made by electronic instruments. Turn to pages 28 and 29 to find out how you can make sound effects of your own from everyday objects.

Scottish percussionist Evelyn Glennie plays concerto for Water, Percussion and Orchestra with the BBC Symphony Orchestra in July 2004.

Rainstick

Rainstick Rainstick

Have you heard the gentle trickling sound of a rainstick? Most rainsticks are made from a hollowed-out tree branch or a bamboo cane. Inside are dried seeds or small stones.

When you turn the tube over, the seeds fall to one end. Turned slowly, the seeds make the trickling sound of rain. Turned quickly, they create a sharper, louder sound.

Today some rainsticks are made from transparent plastic, with pellets inside, which you can watch as they fall from one end to the other.

Did you know?

In ancient times people believed that playing the rainstick would bring rain. Another name for the rainstick is the rattling stick.

This Australian rainstick is decorated with traditional Aboriginal patterns.

Flexatone

Flexatone Flexatone Flexatone

This strange-looking instrument makes an equally strange sound! It was invented about 80 years ago in England.

The player holds the flexatone in one hand and shakes it to make a weird, wailing rattle. The sound comes from a thin metal sheet, which has two wooden knobs on springs attached to it.

When the knobs hit the metal sheet, it makes a high wail. Bending (or flexing) the sheet of metal changes the pitch of the wail.

The metal sheet in the middle of the flexatone makes the note higher or lower when it is pressed.

Rattles Rattles

Rattles Rattles Rattles

Rattles are not just for babies. In ancient times people believed they had magical powers, and they have been played in ceremonies and rituals for thousands of years.

Hundreds of different rattles made from all sorts of materials are played all over the world. You can hear egg-shaped rattles called maracas played in Latin American music. Most maracas are made of wood and have pellets inside which make a soft swishing sound when they are shaken.

This maraca player is taking part in celebrations on the Caribbean island of Haiti.

Gourd rattles are made from dried gourds (a fruit like a small pumpkin). When the gourd is completely dry, the seeds rattle around inside. Gourd rattles from America and Africa are often decorated with carvings or feathers. Some are hollowed out and filled with small stones or shells before being sealed up again.

A Tarahumara Indian in Mexico wears a colourful traditional head-dress as he plays.

Basketwork rattles are made by weaving together thin twigs, canes or willow in different shapes.

The shekere comes from west Africa. It is a hollow gourd with seeds hanging on a net around it. You knock the net against the gourd to play it.

Many South American rattles are made from clay. Rattling cups have a base filled with clay pellets.

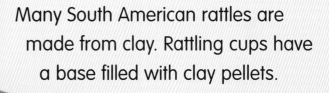

Whip Whip Whip Whip

Have you heard a whip being cracked? A musical whip looks nothing like the whip used by horse riders, but it makes the same sound. Two long pieces of wood are joined at one end by a hinge.

To play the whip, you hold one piece of wood in each hand, and snap them together. This creates the sharp sound of a whip cracking. You can hear the whip in a piece of music called *Young Person's Guide to the Orchestra*. A British composer called Benjamin Britten, wrote it to show the sounds of different instruments.

Did you know?

Another name for the whip is the slapstick or the jazz stick.

A small and a large whip - the larger the pieces of wood, the louder the sound they make.

Wind machine
Wind machine

A wind machine is a drum or barrel on a stand, with a handle at one end. The outer part of the drum has narrow strips of wood stuck to it, which are covered by a piece of silk or canvas.

When the player turns the handle, the drum revolves (turns) and the wood strips rub against the fabric to make a rushing noise like the wind.

The faster the drum turns, the higher the sound the machine makes.

Gong Gong Gong

Most gongs are large, round metal disks hung from a stand. In the middle is a raised part called the boss. Players hit the boss with a wooden stick which has a soft, felt-covered head.

Struck hard, the gong booms loudly as it vibrates. Beaten softly, it makes a gentle, mysterious sound.

Gongs were first played in China about 1,500 years ago. Today they play an important part in a gamelan orchestra, and in music from India, China, Japan and Africa. You can also hear the gong in a western orchestra, where it is called the tam-tam.

A boy touches the huge gong in Mahamuni Pagoda in Myanmar. The gong is 200 years old.

Cog rattle Cog rattle

Did you know?
Cog rattles were once used by farmers to scare birds away from their crops.

When you turn the handle of a cog rattle it makes a loud clacking sound.

Which musical instrument can you hear at a football match? The cog rattle! There are several different types, some made of wood and some of plastic.

A cog rattle has thin strips of wood inside called tongues, and one or two cog wheels attached to the handle. When the rattle is swung round, the tongues make a loud clacking sound as they scrape against the cog wheel.

13

The bull-roarer is one of the oldest instruments in the world. In the Stone Age, people fastened a thin piece of bone to a cord, and whirled it around their heads to create a sound.

Today most bull-roarers are carved from a flat piece of wood, with a hole at one end. The player holds the end of the string and whirls the bull-roarer around his head to make a fluttering roar. Small bull-roarers make a higher sound than large ones.

Bull-roarers are usually carved from wood and decorated with pictures or patterns.

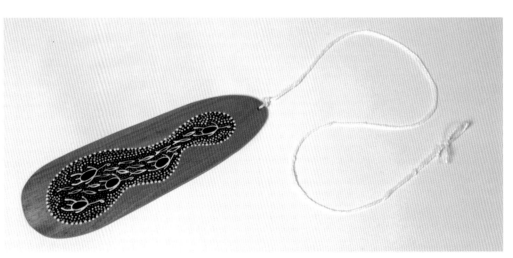

Bull-roarer

The bull-roarer has been played by tribespeople in Africa, Australia, North and South America for thousands of years. Some believe that the instrument has magic powers, that it can conjure up the wind, or that it is the voice of an ancestor or spirit.

Did you know?

Other names for the bull-roarer are the hummer-buzzer, the swish and the thunderstick.

Beautifully decorated bull-roarers from North and South America.

15

Wood blocks

Wood blocks Wood blocks

Wood blocks are exactly that: pieces of wood which players hit with a wooden stick. There are different shapes, but most are made from a rounded, solid block of wood.

Wood blocks were first played in China and were quite large – up to 60 centimetres across.

The wood blocks played in a western orchestra are not so big. Sets of them are lined up in front of the player and hit with a knobbly wooden stick. They are most often used to imitate the sound of horses' hoofs.

The stick used to play the wood blocks has a rounded rubber end.

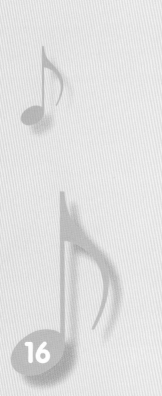

16

Slit drum Slit drum Slit drum

The first slit drums were carved from tree trunks thousands of years ago, and beaten to send messages and signals over long distances.

Today they are made from a length of wood hollowed out through a slit in one side. The drummer beats the drum with his hands or sticks. He can make a variety of sounds by hitting the drum in different places.

Some Pacific Ocean islanders play slit drums which have been carved from tree trunks while they are still rooted to the ground.

A boy carries his slit drum during a peace festival in Kalibo in the Philippines.

The oldest type of bell ever played is called the struck bell, because the player hits (or strikes) it with a beater. This sort of bell was played in China 4,000 years ago and is still played in Eastern music.

Other bells have a pellet or clapper inside them, which sounds when they are moved.

Handbells are metal clapper bells with metal or leather handles. You might hear them played in a group, where the musicians play bells of different sizes to make different notes. The musicians hold a bell in each hand, and sound them by flicking them gently upwards.

The clapper inside this hand bell will sound when it clangs against the bell.

The biggest clapper bell you are likely to hear is a church bell. These huge iron bells can be as big as a person. They are hung inside church-towers and played by bell-ringers, who pull on long bell-ropes hanging down from the bell.

A monk holds a handbell with a decorated handle.

This Mexican boy is about to ring a church bell in Baja California, Mexico.

Bells Bells Bells Bells

Agogo bells Agogo bells

These bells make a clear, bright ringing sound. They are struck bells, which you play by hitting them, as they do not have a clapper inside.

Agogo bells are two metal cone-shapes joined together by a curved metal handle. The two bells sound different notes when you strike them with a metal rod. They come in several different sizes.

Agogo bells originally came from Africa, but you most often hear them played in Latin American bands today.

Agogo bells do not have clappers inside, but are hit with a metal rod to make them sound.

Agogo bells

20

Jingles

Jingles are tiny round bells with hard pellets inside, attached to a frame made of wood, metal or plastic. When shaken, they make a high, tinkling sound.

Thousands of years ago, people sewed jingles on their clothes, and to the bridles of their horses. They believed that the jingles would frighten away evil spirits.

In South America and Africa jingles are made from nuts or shells. They are worn as necklaces, belts or anklets, or attached to a stick and played in dances and ceremonies.

An Indian folk dancer in Jaipur wears bells around his ankles.

Did you know?
The Christmas song 'Jingle Bells' is about riding on a sleigh with jingles attached to it.

Cabasa Cabasa
Cabasa   Cabasa

To play the cabasa, you hold the handle in one hand and twist the beads around with the other.

The casaba is a rattle with steel beads strung around the outside.

You can hear the cabasa playing the rhythm in South American dance bands. The percussionist holds the rattle in one hand, and twists the beads around it with the other. The beads rub across metal ridges underneath to make a scraping sound.

Early cabasas were made from gourds (a fruit like a small pumpkin) covered with netting which was threaded with wooden beads.

Washboard

This washboard is part of a one-woman band in New Orleans, Louisiana, USA.

Washboard players look as though they are wearing a large metal bib.

A washboard is a metal or wooden board with ridges running from side to side. Washboard players wear metal thimbles over their fingers, which they scrape over the ridges.

Some players use a short metal bar to make the washboard's sharp, rhythmic sound.

Did you know?

Before people had electric washing machines they used washboards to scrub dirty clothes, which they rubbed up and down over the ridges.

Theremin Theremin
Theremin Theremin

Y ou don't have to touch this instrument to play it! It is a wooden box with an aerial at the top and a metal loop in the side.

To make a sound, the player moves one hand around in front of the aerial. There is a magnetic field around the aerial. When the player's hand moves into it, the theremin gives a wailing sound. The player's other hand moves over the metal loop, which makes the sound louder or softer.

This strange instrument was invented by a Russian called Lev Theremin 80 years ago. It is very hard to play!

Lev Theremin plays the instrument he invented, which was named after him.

24

Thunder sheet

The thunder sheet was first created as a special sound effect in theatres. Today it can create a fantastically noisy rumbling sound in the percussion section of an orchestra.

A thunder sheet is made of thin steel and hung on a stand. The percussionist shakes it by hand, or hits it with a soft beater. Most thunder sheets are about 3.65 metres high and 1.2 metres wide, but they can be much smaller or larger.

Did you know?

A sound like thunder can also be made by dropping heavy metal balls on to leather, or by rolling the balls down a wooden slope. Today, most thunder sounds are tape recordings of real thunder.

This percussionist is about to make a sound like thunder with his thunder sheet.

Anvil Anvil Anvil Anvil

Before cars were invented many people travelled on horseback. Heavy metal anvils were used by blacksmiths to make shoes for the horses. They took a lump of red hot iron, and beat it with a hammer on their anvil into the shape of a horseshoe. The shoes were nailed to the bottom of the horses' hoofs to protect them.

Today, the sound of a hammer clanging heavily on a metal anvil can occasionally be heard as a special effect in a western orchestra. Several anvils are played during an opera called *Il Trovatore*, by the Italian composer Giuseppe Verdi.

This traditional anvil is played by beating it with hammers.

Kazoo Kazoo Kazoo Kazoo

Do you play the kazoo? When you hum into it, the air from your mouth vibrates against a thin piece of paper, called a membrane, and makes a buzzing sound.

Most kazoos today are plastic and are sold as toys, but 70 years ago there were kazoo bands in parts of Europe.

Kazoos belong to a group of instruments called the mirliton family. All have a membrane inside, which changes the note the musician hums into a buzzing sound.

Did you know?

Another name for the kazoo is Tommy Talker. You can make your own mirliton by putting a piece of tissue paper over a comb and humming against it.

A family hum into their kazoos together. The kazoo turns the note into a buzzing sound.

Do-it-yourself sound effects

Y ou can make an amazing range of sound effects using everyday objects.

See if you can find six glasses that are exactly the same. Fill each one with a different amount of water, starting with very little and rising to an almost full glass. Try playing tunes by tapping the glasses with a metal spoon.

You can do the same thing with identical bottles filled with different amounts of water. You can also play bottles by blowing gently across the open top to sound a note.

Did you know?

In October 2000, two flute-players from Ohio created the largest bottle orchestra ever. Patricia Rentner and Roselyn Smith played various nursery rhymes on 470 bottles.

Fill identical bottles with different amounts of water, then tap them with a metal spoon.

Try gently wiping a wet finger around the rim of a wine glass. The thinner the glass, the easier this is. Your finger causes vibrations in the bowl of the glass, which makes the sound.

Rattles can be made from empty cans. Wash them well, then fill them with dried beans. Tape cardboard or paper over the open ends and shake.

Start a stone collection, arranging them according to the note they make when you hit them with a smaller stone. Shells, nuts and small pieces of wood also make a sound if you rub or clack them together.

A street musician in Paris rubs his fingers around the rims of wine glasses to make music.

29

Words to remember

bamboo A tall grass with a hollow stem.

band A group of musicians playing together.

beaters Wooden or wire sticks used to tap or hit some instruments.

clapper A small piece of metal inside a bell which strikes the sides of the bell to make it sound.

composer Someone who writes pieces of music.

gamelan orchestra A group of instruments from Indonesia played during religious ceremonies. It can include percussion instruments, drums, fiddles and flutes.

musician Someone who plays an instrument or sings.

opera A play which is sung. The first opera was written in Italy around 1600. An orchestra accompanies (plays alongside) the singers and provides background music.

orchestra A large group of about 90 musicians playing classical music together. Serious music is sometimes called classical music to separate it from popular music. Classical music can also mean music which was written during the late 18th and early 19th centuries and followed certain rules.

pellet A tiny ball made of metal or other hard material.

percussionist Someone who plays a percussion instrument.

pitch How low or high a sound is.

rhythm The beat of the music, which depends on how short or long the notes are.

ritual A series of actions carried out in a particular way, according to the custom of a society or group.

soundtrack Music which accompanies a television programme or film.

tam-tam The name for a gong played in a western orchestra.

thimble A small metal cap worn on a finger.

tongue A thin strip of wood

vibrate To move up and down very quickly, or quiver.

Index